From the Books of

Iconographia

a Franco Maria Ricci edition

COTTON AND SILK MAKING

in Manchu China

Introduction by
Mario Bussagli
Excerpts from
Father J.-B. Du Halde S.J.

RIZZOLI NEW YORK

The publisher would like to thank the Bibliothèque Nationale of Paris and the Biblioteca Nazionale of Florence for their kind collaboration, Sebastiana Papa for her photographs and Gianni Guadalupi for his arrangement of the texts.

Designed by Franco Maria Ricci
Edited by Laura Casalis and Gianni Guadalupi
Translated from the Italian and the French by Michael Langley
Photographs by Sebastiana Papa
Colour separations by Fotoincisa Reprolit, Parma
Text composed in Bodoni Italics
Printed in Milan by GEA S.p.A., February 1980
Published in the United States of America by
RIZZOLI INTERNATIONAL PUBLICATIONS, INC.
712 Fifth Avenue/New York 10019

Library of Congress Catalog Card Number: 79-93005
ISBN: 0-8478-0306-6
Printed in Italy

Introduction

The production phases and methods for working silk in old China are illustrated with great accuracy in the two series of album leaves shown here. Although it is not possible to date them exactly, both are of the period starting at the turn of the XVIIth century and ending in about 1850. In other words, they appeared under the Manchu or Ch'ing Dynasty and were therefore influenced by the trend towards encyclopaedism and detailed information which reached its peak under the Emperor K'ang-hsi (1662-1722).

In 1728 this ruler announced the famous "Collection of books and ancient and modern illustrations" (Ku chin t'u-shu chi-ch'eng) *which was edited at his command in six sections: celestial phenomena, geography, human relations, sciences and arts, literature, political economy. Its 11995 sub-sections covered every branch of knowledge and kept a vast number of scholars busy for many years. The "Collection" was the sequel to a great dictionary called the* K'ang-hsi tzu-tien *which had appeared in 1716. With its two supplements this dictionary, which contains 49030 ideograms, is still considered essential to the study of Chinese poetry, itself a vast and wide-ranging subject.*

The diffusion of useful knowledge in illustrated form is not an exclusively western heritage. Interest in manufacturing methods for materials in common use is not to be ascribed solely to the Age of Enlightenment in Europe, a continent which, under the cultural lead of France, had exalted Confucius, the man of reason, to the skies, so that he was to become the "patron saint" of the XVIIIth century in all but name. It is to the spirit of this period, steeped as it was in analogies, affinities and convergencies of two "worlds" different and distant from one another, that our illustrative material belongs.

The eighteen rice paper colour plates describing the methods of cultivating, preparing and weaving cotton are contained in an album (24 × 32 cms) bound in red silk which is preserved in the Bibliothèque Nationale *in Paris (B.N.0e 97). They show how this highly important textile fibre was produced and worked, with the reminder that it was not only intended for the poor and needy but also for state officials. For practical reasons certain garments betokening rank and importance sometimes had to be made in cotton or cotton gauze.*

The twenty-three coloured engravings showing the breeding of silk-worms and the working of raw silk come from a paperboard album (25 × 32 cms) which is in the keeping of the National Library, Florence (Banco Rari 76). There is a similar copy in the Bibliothèque Nationale, *Paris (B.N.Oe 89). They depict the typically Chinese art of producing silk, a material which for a very long time was the hallmark that distinguished this people — at least in the eyes of the Chinese of Chung-kuo "the middle country", who saw themselves as the centre of the Universe — from those barbarians who knew and appreciated silk but did not know how to cultivate it.*

Taken as a whole, these illustrations do not belong to the great tradition of courtly painting or to that of fine graphic representation. Nor are they of that popular genre which included subjects motivated by the theatre, by decorative art and by the exchange of respects and greetings. Their circulation ran into figures that are startling even by modern standards, tens of millions of copies per year coming from single production centres which issued them in series grouped by motifs.

Our illustrations are essentially informative and belong to a group in themselves. The silk series has its origin in early lithographic engravings that date back to the XIIIth century and were re-interpreted in 1696 by the Court painter Ts'ao Ping-cheng at the orders of the Emperor K'ang-hsi. To give them descriptive clarity many of the plates present broad views of the landscape executed with elegance and economy of line. At the same time reminders are everywhere present of the western approach to perspective, particularly in the interior scenes. When human figures appear it is as an adjunct necessary to the working surroundings, therefore they are given far more stress than is usual in courtly paintings. In the latter every emphasis was placed on the overwhelming splendour of nature in comparison with Man and his works, these being symbolised proportionally to the almost negligible degree of importance that was attached to ordinary human activities.

None the less, our album pictures have antecedents — ancestors, we might almost say — of illustrious fame. In various ways, whether it be in a certain likeness of didactic content or in some link that is not easy to define historically, we would claim Ku k'ai-chih (A.D. 344 - 406) as an important ancestor of these works. His scroll entitled "Admonitions of the Instructress to the Court Ladies" depicts scenes that call for the utmost care in the portrayal of expression, gestures, movements, clothes and other details of feminine character. Ku k'ai-chih is not only one of the most ancient of the great Chinese painters to leave a memorable mark, he was the first to leave work that enables us to understand the reasons underlying it. With him the explanatory, instructive aim was undoubtedly predominant, and, only slightly less so, his exceptional interest in female imagery. On this basis alone the master was able to suppress the background, reducing it to an atmosphere punctuated by common objects, by vibrant body movements, by the very background of the unbleached silk on which he painted. In a like manner, but with a more insistent explanatory need behind it, similar solutions were introduced into our illustrations, with the difference that the latter present figures that are much less graceful than Ku K'ai-chi's nymphs and damsels. Moreover, the example of European prints, of their aesthetic quality and instructive merit, is as clearly evident in the perspective of geometrical forms as in the studied arrangement of human figures. For the purpose of these figures was to show the nature of the work that was being illustrated, how it was done and what still had to be done in order to complete the product, the uses of which might then be explained pictorially. In these images man poses no philosophical or religious problems. He appears as homo faber pure and simple, Man the creator, calmly and methodically performing tasks of which he is the complete master. He is anything but a robot, anything but a bondsman or disgruntled wage slave. He gives the impression of being an exemplary model of the craftsman's skill.

On going through this book looking page by page a the various phases depicted, we cannot help wondering if the self-same characters follow us along while tackling their respective jobs, or whether each separate phase was entrusted to an artist familiar with one aspect only of the production cycle. The answer must be left to the imagination aided by technical references found in the text.

Turning to the problem of perspective, it should not be forgotten that this illustrative work belongs to a period when China was showing lively curiosity in the illusory capacity of western perspective. In response to this surge of interest Father Buglio had *written his important* Treatise on Perspective *in Chinese. Another contribution to the subject was made by Father Giuseppe Castiglione, a Milanese who worked in China from 1715 to 1768 under the name of Lang Shih-ning. In an attempt to reconcile the European and Chinese techniques he created a hybrid method which in many respects was more Chinese than European. But in the case of our illustrations the instructive aim and the need for clarity were to give them that vaguely occidental look which is somewhat out of place because it is anti-traditional, at least from the Chinese point of view.Besides, it was tied in with schematic principles which, as Castiglione was to find out to his cost, were not easily understood by master masons, artisans and working people in China. One plan for the construction of a pavilion which Castiglione presented in axonometric projection proved so incomprehensible to the builders — they could not "read" it — that Castiglione and a Jesuit colleague had to design it all over again in a form understandable to the craftsmen.*

This shows that our illustrations were not intended for technicians but for persons who knew little or nothing about the operations described, for the dilettanti of social strata more amenable to western influences and for whom the new approach was likely to prove edifying. In short, they were really meant for the upper classes. And this development is an echo of what happened with the great French Encyclopaedia of that day. It was most appreciated precisely by those classes whom it sought to disparage, by those who were better equipped to understand the use and significance of its information and methodical explanations than were those who should have referred to it for information and ideas essential to their work.

Mario Bussagli

Cotton

The cultivation of cotton came late to China, probably in the XIIth century A.D., although there are some who believe that it was grown there as much as two centuries earlier. The Arab Suleiman, who visited China in the IXth century, spoke of silk as the material that was used for the clothes of rich and poor alike, but he made no mention of cotton. The great Marco Polo, who was in China in about 1290, devotes several passages to cotton growing in Persia, Malabar and Bengal, but not in his chapters on the Middle Kingdom.

It was in the north-west provinces that cotton cultivation began, but because of opposition from the producers of silk and hemp it was slow to spread and did not become general until the latter years of the Yüan Dynasty (1276-1365). At the time when our illustrations were engraved China's great cotton-growing region was the Valley of the Yangtze, the "blue river" of the missionaries. And it is located there to this day.

The soil was first treated with muddy silt from the beds of irrigation channels. This was mixed with ash and spread over the ploughed fields. Then, towards the end of April, the crop was sown. When the shoots appeared the seedlings were transplanted, five or six at a time, into single holes, where they were lightly dusted with ash and, if necessary, hoed. During their growth the young plants were thinned out, weeds were removed, and this went on until the flowers began to blossom in late July or early August. Then, when the capsules, or seed-vessels, ripened and opened shortly before they would normally begin to fall, the cultivator picked them and separated the cotton from the seeds and their sheaths.

Weather was obviously an important factor. A really hot summer's day or a rainy spell in autumn could ruin the crop. Thus August to October, when the capsules were ripening, was the crucial period. If all went well, the seeds were separated from the fibre by a special appliance fitted with rollers. The peasant growers would then sell their raw cotton to the city merchants who would have it spun, made into skeins, combed and sent off to the looms on which it was woven.

Silk

From Father Jean-Baptiste Du Halde's *Description of the Empire of China and of Chinese Tartary* (ed. 1735)

[...] *It was from Greece that Europe received the gift o silk, which in the days of the Roman empire was worth its weight in gold. The Greeks owed it to the Persians... who own that it was from China that they first learned the art of rearing silkworms.*

To find other references to silk as remote in time as those relating to China would indeed be difficult. The most ancient writers of that empire attribute its discovery to one of the wives of the Emperor Huang ti. She was called Si ling and later, as a mark of honour, Yuen fei.

Before the time of this queen, when Chinese agriculture was in its earliest stages, people wore th skins of animals. As the inhabitants increased in number the supply of skins became insufficient. Neec forced the people to be industrious and they started weaving fibres in order to cover themselves. But it was to the lady whom we have already mentioned that they owed the discovery of silk.

In later years the empresses made it their gracious duty to see that the larvae of silkworms were hatched, that the worms were fed and reared and their silk collected and woven. The royal palace hac a special orchard for the cultivation of mulberry trees. Accompanied by ladies of the court, the empress would go to this orchard and ceremoniousl pick the leaves from three branches which the members of the retinue would hold within her reach The finest pieces of silk, woven by herself, or at her orders and in her presence, were reserved for the great sacrificial ceremony in honour of Chang li.

It is clear that the empresses gave this matter their

attention for political reasons. They wished, by their example, to encourage the princesses, the ladies of rank and the people in general to rear silkworms. Similarly, to promote agriculture and to urge their subjects to the performance of thankless tasks, with the coming of spring the emperors never failed to turn their hand to the plough, ceremoniously ploughing a few furrows and scattering them with seed. Even now the reigning emperor maintains this custom. [...]

The truth is that China is the country of silk, for it would seem to be inexhaustible. As well as to many countries of Asia and Europe, it is supplied to the emperor, to princes, courtiers, mandarins, men of letters, ladies and, in general, to all who have the means to pay for it. They wear clothes of satin or damask; only the lower classes and the peasants wear cotton clothes dyed blue. In this empire excellent silk is produced in many provinces, but the best — and it is incomparably fine — comes from the province of Tche kiang.

The Chinese judge their silk by its whiteness, its softness and its fineness. If it is at all rough to the touch, that is a bad sign, in which case to improve its appearance they often treat it with a special rice water mixed with burning lime. As a result, when it is transported to Europe this silk must not be wetted. Not so with pure silk, than which there is nothing easier to wring and twist. The Chinese workman does so for an hour at a time without stopping, which means without breaking a single thread. There exists nothing smoother or more beautiful than spun silk. The frames that the Chinese use when reeling, that is unwinding, their silk are very different from any used in Europe, and far less cumbersome. They consist in two or three bamboo skein-winders with wooden crosspieces. How surprising to see with what simple instruments they make these lovely fabrics! [...]

The silks most commonly used in China are in single colours or with floral designs, and these are for summer clothes. The Chinese make damasks of all kinds and all colours: striped satins and the black satins of Nan king, coarse-grained taffetas and watered moirés. They also produce various kinds of taffeta: some with floral designs like those of Tours, others that resemble gauze adorned with bright flowers. Many fabrics are made with stripes of exquisite elegance, or else veined as moiré is or dotted over with little roses. Also crêpes, brocades, heavy stuffs and different types of velvet. Of the last named, the crimson shades are most highly esteemed, but they can be imitated. One way to discover whether this has been done is to take some lemon juice mixed with lime and sprinkle a few drops on the fabric. If the colour changes the material is false. Then there are those other qualities of silk that the Chinese make which are unknown in Europe. Two, in particular, are very popular in China.

The first is a kind of satin which is stronger and glossier than European satin and is called Touan tse. It is sometimes made in single colours, sometimes with patterns of flowers, trees, birds and butterflies. The second is a special taffeta called Tcheou tse with which underclothing and linings are made. This material is close-woven, yet it is so pliant that it can be folded or rumpled without creasing. It washes like ordinary cloth and does not lose its lustre.

The Chinese workmen give the sheen to Tcheou tse taffeta by using the fat of a freshwater seal called Kiang tchu, which is the "river pig" of the Yang tse kiang. In this great river seals that are smaller than those of the sea are seen more than sixty leagues upstream swimming in shoals one behind the other, leaping and performing antics just as they do in open waters. The fat of these seals is purified by washing and cooking. A fine brush is taken and the fat is spread in layers on the taffeta, working from

the top downwards but only on the side requiring a lustrous finish. When working at night the men use this melted seal fat for their lamps instead of oil. Its smell drives away flies from the workshop, which is most convenient because these insects settle on the woven silk and damage it very considerably. [...]
In the province of Chan tong a special silk is produced with which a fabric called Kien tcheou is made. The worms which secrete this silk are of two kinds: a large, dark species known as Tfouen kien, and a smaller one called Tiao kien. The cocoon of the first is reddish grey, of the second almost black. The thread from them, which is of the two colours just mentioned, is close-packed, does not break, lasts well and washes like ordinary cloth. If the quality is good it does not absorb stains, even those of oil. This fabric is highly esteemed by the Chinese and sometimes costs as much as satin and the best quality weaves. But since the Chinese are extremely clever at the art of counterfeit they produce a false type of Kien tcheou with waste silk of the Tche kiang variety. Those who are not on their guard will be easily taken in. For some years now the people of Canton have been manufacturing stockings, ribbons and buttons made of silk, and with the most excellent results. Their silk stockings cost one tael, or a little less, and the largest buttons about ten sous a dozen.
Because silk depends for its abundance and quality on the way the worms are reared and on the care with which they are fed from the time of hatching until they spin their cocoons, it may be both useful and interesting to describe the Chinese methods of production. A famous writer of the Ming Dynasty, who lived in a province where silk was plentiful, compiled a weighty tome on this subject, and Father Dentrecolles has sent me an extract from that book. I quote here what seems to me most relevant for the perfection of so fine a trade, and for ensuring its success. And since silk is not dear in China the expense necessary to embark on this activity is not great. Besides, the high regard for silk in Europe, whence many ships sail every year to seek new supplies, leads us to believe that the knowledge of the Chinese on so fascinating a matter cannot but be useful.

(Extract from an old Chinese book showing how silkworms should be reared and fed in order to obtain a better and more abundant output.)
[...] *Avoid those mulberry trees that shed their fruit before their leaves, for such leaves are usually very small and unhealthy. Moreover, this kind of tree is short-lived and withers away in a very few years. When choosing saplings, ignore those that have a rough bark as they produce leaves that are too small and fine. On the contrary, select trees with a white bark, few knots and strong side-shoots. These will yield large, thick leaves, and the worms that feed on them will in due course produce tightly packed cocoons that are rich in silk. The best mulberry trees are those with few berries on them, since their juice goes mostly to the leaves. Here, then, is a way to propagate more leaves by rendering the fruit sterile: take freshly picked or sun-dried berries and feed them to chickens; collect the excrement of the chickens, dissolve it in water, soak mulberry seed in this water and then sow it.*
[...]
With some trees the leaves sprout early: those that grow near houses do so. In order to protect their roots from weeds, use manure, water them during dry spells, and keep a first supply of food ready for the newly hatched insects. [...]
The best soil in which to grow mulberry trees is neither too strong nor too hard. A field that has been freshly tilled after remaining fallow for a long period is most suitable. In the provinces of Tche kiang and Kiang nan, where the best silk comes from, care is taken to manure the ground with mud

dredged from channels that thread the countryside and are cleaned every year. The ash and excrement of animals, including that of silkworms, can also be used for manure. Small vegetables growing between the mulberry trees do no harm, provided always that the soil is not hoed too close to the trees lest the roots be damaged.

Most important — and this is a matter of great advantage — is to see that the mulberry trees are pruned by a skilled hand, and in accordance with the rules of that art. The tree will then come into leaf early and abundantly, and its leaves, which are most nutritious, will rouse the silkworm's appetite. Do not be afraid of thinning out the branches excessively, especially those at the centre of the tree where an empty and suitable place should be left free. From this place in the tree the picker can then collect the leaves more easily. And he will pick more leaves in a single day than one who has not taken this precaution will pick in a whole week. A mulberry tree well pruned is worth two that have not been thinned out. [...]

It is not enough merely to cultivate the trees to supply food for the worms. It is also necessary to prepare a place to accommodate these insects in their various stages of development during the time they take to complete their work. These remarkable creatures contribute to the luxury and beauty of our clothes and houses and deserve to be treated with proper regard. Moreover, the quality of their product is according to the care that is given to them, for if they suffer and languish their silk will suffer and languish too. [...]

It is necessary, says one author, to choose a pleasant spot on which to rear the silkworms, and to see that it is on raised ground, that it is dry, yet not too far from a stream. The larvae have to be dipped and rinsed quite frequently and running water is best for this. The shed should be built in a place apart, with no stables nearby, no dunghills, no

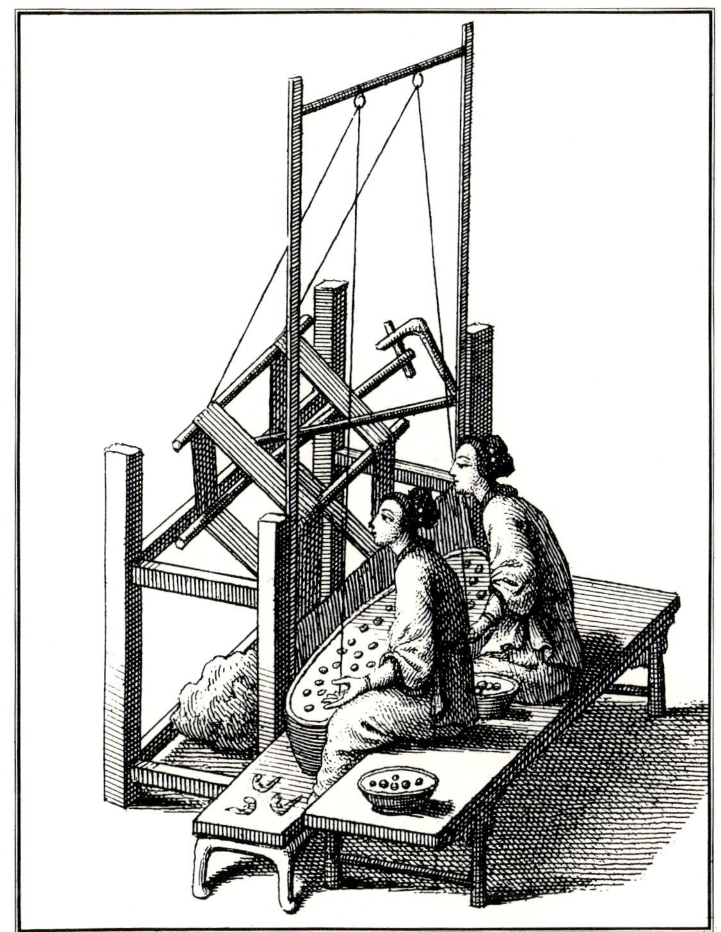

drains, no noise. Foul smells and startling noises have a strange effect on these delicate creatures. The bark of a dog or the penetrating crow of a cock is enough to upset them when they have just emerged from the larvae.

The shed should be a square one such as can be used for other purposes when the silkworm season is over. As the air must be kept slightly warm, the walls should be well-made with the entrance facing south, or south-east, but never towards the north. There should be four windows, one on each wall, to admit air freely whenever there is need. These windows, which are almost always kept closed, should consist of white transparent paper, for light must be let in at times while at other times the room must remain in darkness. It is therefore convenient

to keep some portable mats at hand. [...]
It is important that the larvae should all hatch at the same time and that the silkworms sleep, stay awake, eat and go through their transformation stage contemporaneously. For this reason alone an even and constant degree of warmth should always be maintained in their shed. [...]
The question then arises of fitting out the shed and of preparing the necessary instruments to provide for the needs of the silkworms. Nine or ten wooden shelves are mounted one above the other with a space of about nine inches between each. These are set with a mesh of rushes loosely interwoven so that the little finger can pass through the joints, for the warm fresh air must enter. This structure is placed round the walls, but with room enough to be able to work on both sides. It is on these large-mesh rush mats that the larvae hatch and the worms feed until they are ready to spin their silk cocoons.
The rush mats form the cradle for these extremely delicate insects, and to this cradle a kind of mattress is added consisting of a layer of dry, chopped straw over which a long sheet of paper is spread. When the paper is soiled with excreta it is covered with a mesh the holes of which allow the worms to pass. This mesh is spread with fresh mulberry leaves whose smell attracts the hungry worms to it so that they quickly climb through. Later it is carefully lifted and placed on a clean rush mesh. The dirty one is removed for cleaning, after which it will be used again. [...]
Here now are the tasks to be performed during the three days preceding the birth of the silkworms, for it is most important that the larvae should all hatch at the same time. When birth is imminent the egg is seen to swell and to become slightly pointed. On the first of the three days, at ten or eleven o'clock when the sky is clear and, as is normal at that season, a light breeze is blowing, the paper scrolls on which the eggs have been kept are taken from their containers. They are unrolled, hung out back to the sun and left there until the temperature begins to warm up. Then they are rolled up again, quite tightly, and returned to their containers or put in a warm place until the following day, when the same operation is repeated. By now the larvae have changed colour to an ashen grey. The scrolls should then be joined together in pairs, rolled up, more tightly this time, and fastened at the ends.
Towards evening on the third day the scrolls are unrolled and spread out on mats. It will now be seen that the larvae are almost black. If any worms have already appeared they should be thrown away, for experience teaches us that these are never of a communal type, they will never harmonize with the others in the rhythms of transformation, of feeding and, above all, of spinning their cocoons. These eccentrics cause so much embarrassment, so many losses, that it is best to get rid of them immediately. When they have been removed the scrolls are re-rolled, three at a time, and put in a warm place sheltered from the south wind. At about ten or eleven o'clock on the following day they are once again unrolled and found to be full of silkworms that look like black ants. That, in fact, is what they call them: He Y. *If, within the next hour, any eggs remain unhatched, then these must be discarded. And if among those that have hatched there are any with flat heads, or a withered or burnt-up look, or any blue, yellow or flesh-pink ones, these too must be rejected. The best have the same colour as a mountain has when seen from a distance.*
Most advisable is it to weigh the paper on which the newborn silkworms have been placed. The sheet is then turned upside down over another one which has been spread with mulberry leaves to attract the hungry insects by their smell. If any worms are drowsy, help them to move with the feather of a chicken or by tapping softly on the back of the paper. The empty sheet is weighed again so that the

exact weight of the silkworms can be ascertained. This is done in order to calculate what weight of leaves will be required for feeding the worms, and from that what weight of cocoons can be expected if all goes well.

Arrangements must now be made for enabling the silkworms to follow their diet and for keeping the room at the right temperature. For this purpose a mother is found who will watch over the worms with affection and attend to their needs. She is called Tsan mou, the silkworm mother. After washing herself throughly and putting on clothes that are clean and free of all bad smells, she takes possession of the shed. She should not have eaten just before, nor should she have handled wild chicory, for the smell of this plant is prejudicial to the tender brood. The better to judge the warmth of the room she should wear simple clothes that do not fold around her, and she should stir up or damp down the fire as and when necessary. But she should take heed never to allow any smoke to get into the room or set up a dust. Such conditions are most harmful to these tiny delicate creatures which have to be treated with the utmost care before their time of transformation comes. Every day is like a whole year for them, one writer tells us.: the four seasons are morning, which is their Spring, midday their Summer, evening their Autumn, and night their Winter. [...]

When the silkworms are ready to go to work, it can be so arranged that they make a small thin piece of silk, which is flat and round like a sacramental wafer, instead of spinning cocoons in the usual manner. All that is required is to cover a small wafer-shaped container with a piece of paper of exactly the same size. The insect is then put inside to spin its silk. There are several advantages in this method.

First, the flat, round pices unwind, or "reel", just as easily as do cocoons. Secondly, the silk is so pure

and free from that humid stickiness which silkworms leave in their cocoons, and which the Chinese say is their urine. With its work finished, the insect is removed before it has time to soil it. Thirdly, there is no need to reel the silk soon after it has been spun, as must be done with cocoons. Reeling can be delayed without risk for as long as is necessary. Once this has been done the Chinese think only of making the best use they can of their silk, and for this purpose they employ the simplest of instruments. It is hardly possible to describe them briefly and clearly. They are better understood by looking at them than by reading about them. And that is why the various devices and mechanisms which the Chinese use when making the beautiful silks they send to Europe are shown here as illustrations. [...]

棉 *Cotton Making in Old China*

The Plates are reproduced from the originals in the National Library, Paris, Oe 97.

I - Sowing cotton seed.
II - The young plants are watered.
III - Picking the cotton.
IV - Preparing cotton lint.
V - Spreading lint on a work bench.
VI - Cotton carding.
VII - Reeling carded cotton.
VIII - The reels are made into skeins.
IX - Washing the skeins.
X - Starching the skeins.
XI - The skeins are steam heated.
XII - Drying the skeins.
XIII - The skeins are unwound on to large reels.
XIV - Unwinding cotton to prepare the yarn.
XV - Rolling a ball of yarn before making the warp.
XVI - Combing cotton yarn with an "ouzot".
XVII - Removing superfluous starch from the warp with a wet brush.
XVIII - Weaving cotton fabric on a wooden frame.

絲 *Silk Making in Old China*

The Plates are reproduced from the originals in the National Library, Florence, Banco Rari 76.

I - The eggs, or larvae, are selected with great care. Silkworms sleep, eat and work as a harmonious body and must not be disturbed while hatching.
II - Rejected larvae are buried underground where they cannot tempt domestic animals which suffer harmful effects from eating them. Alternatively, they are thrown to the fishes which thrive on them.
III - Larvae selected for breeding purposes are weighed, then distributed uniformly on specially prepared mats.
IV - It is important that the quarters reserved for silk-worms should be kept at an even temperature as these insects are sensitive to atmospheric changes. On cold days braziers are lit to warm the air.
V - Collecting mulberry leaves which form the sole diet of these hungry creatures.
VI - The mulberry leaves are taken to the silkworm farm for selection.
VII - The leaves are shredded into small pieces and spread on mats of meshed rushes for the insects to feed on.
VIII - Silkworms require careful and frequent attention because they sicken easily and resent being disturbed.
IX - The rush meshes have to be cleaned regularly if the insects, which are accustomed to a healthy natural environment, are to work properly.
X - When the silkworms reach maturity they are moved to other mats to give them more space in which to develop their cocoons.
XI - It takes about one week for a silkworm to spin its cocoon. At this stage special care must be taken, day and night, to see that nothing goes wrong.
XII - The cocoons are sorted and those selected for future breeding purposes are stored in a cool, well-aired room.
XIII - Cocoons from which the silk is to be taken are put into earthen jars and covered with layers of leaves and salt to kill off the insects without damaging the silk fibres.
XIV - After soaking them in copper pots filled with hot water the cocoons are unwound.
XV - Dyeing skeins of raw silk.
XVI - Silk cultivators giving thanks to their ancestors at the end of the season.
XVII - The skeins of raw silk are unwound and made into reels.
XVIII - Another device for reeling silk.
XIX - The warp is prepared on this appliance.
XX - Tea being brought to a silk weaver.
XXI - Watching a silk weaver at work.
XXII - Bales of silk in various colours.
XXIII - The silk is brought to the tailors and cutters who make clothes of it at their work bench.

棉

花種

II

III

IV

仁

V

VI

茶

VII

VIII

IX

紗

X

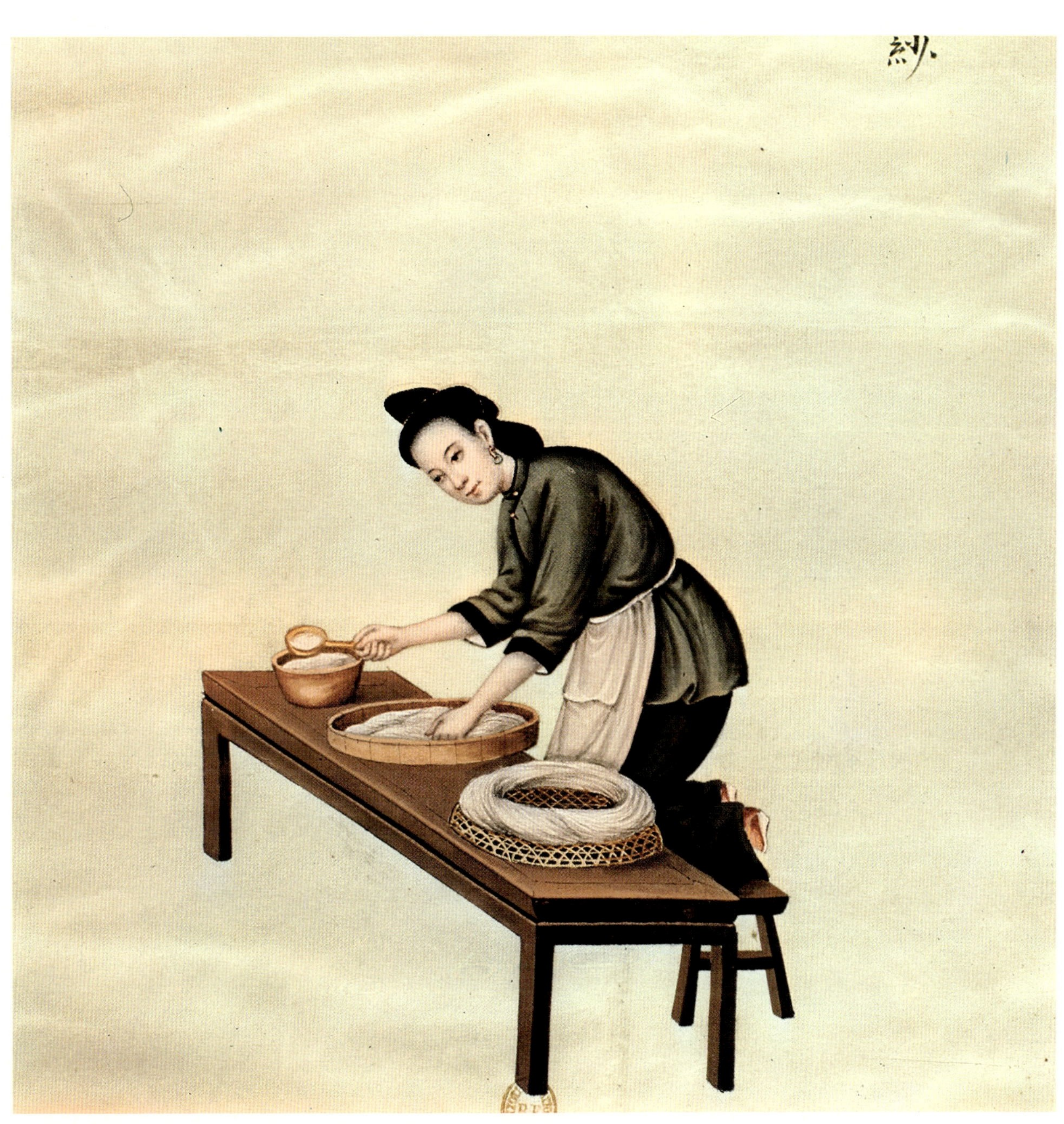

XI

XII

XIII

XIV

XV

R.F.

XVI

XVIII

絲

I

II

III

IV

V

VI

VII

VIII

IX

X

XI

XII

XIII

XIV

XV

XVII

XIX

XX

XXI

XXIII